Alfred Danner

Microwave Cooking

Cookery Editor Sonia Allison

Series Editor Wendy Hobson

foulsham

Foreword

Our high-tech age has produced all manner of clever gadgets and gimmickry for the kitchen but still up there at number one is the microwave oven with its knack of speeding up lengthy cooking times, reducing energy levels, cutting down on washing-up and helping to conserve food nutrients, colour, texture and flavour.

For the most part, the microwave is not a total substitute for a conventional cooker — no hob for stewing, steaming, frying and boiling — though some of the more expensive models do almost everything: defrost, microwave, grill, bake, or work in combination, enabling you to roast and microwave in one operation. When you think about it, a remarkable achievement and feat of scientific ingenuity.

If you are newcomer to microwave cooking, you will find this book of immense help as you come to terms with what is, after all, a fresh and innovative approach to cooking. If you are already a microwave user, you will find a host of new and inventive recipes. I wish you every success.

Contents

Your Microwave Oven

Microwave ovens are no longer new – they are an essential part of the modern kitchen. But many people fall far short of utilising them to their full potential and therefore reaping all the benefits of this efficient way of cooking. If you learn a little more about your microwave, you will soon see how many ways you can use it in your cooking.

Using your Microwave

How Microwaves Work

When the microwave is plugged into a socket, the door closed and the oven switched on, microwaves are emitted from a magnetron (or microwave energy generator) usually at the top of the oven and placed to one side. The magnetron is protected by a cover, generally plastic. The microwaves are transmitted into the inside of the oven cavity down a channel called a waveguide, bounce off the sides, and beam on to the food from all directions. Instantaneously, the food absorbs the microwaves which in turn causes the water molecules within the food itself to vibrate frantically at 2400 million cycles or vibrations per second. The result is excessively rapid friction which creates enough heat to cook food quickly, effectively and cleanly. For a simple comparison of how friction makes heat, rub your hands together vigorously and feel how warm they become. Now multiply this umpteen times and you will understand how the microwaves work. For even cooking, most models are fitted inside with what is called either a wave stirrer, stirrer blade or paddle which helps to distribute the waves. Most models also have a rotating turntable.

Successful Cooking

Microwaves are only able to penetrate 2.5 cm/1 in of the food in all directions. The heat then travels into the centre of the food. It is therefore important to use the correct size and shape of dish in which to cook the food. Shallow, round dishes are usually the most efficient.

Food will also cook more satisfactorily if thick pieces are placed towards the outside edges of the dish and never piled up. Whole potatoes and other similar shaped foods should be arranged in a ring around the outside of a plate or dish. Stirring during the cooking helps to distribute the heat and ensure that everything is evenly cooked.

Resting and Standing Times

In order for heat to penetrate the food and work its way from the outside to the centre, food cooked in a microwave needs to rest or stand at some stages during or after cooking. If some dishes were cooked without a rest, the outside would be overcooked and the middle remain uncooked. Because you can easily spoil a dish by overcooking, it is better to undercook a dish then return it briefly to the oven if necessary.

Seasonings

As salt tends to toughen meat, poultry and offal cooked in a microwave, it should be added at the end of cooking, or half way through. Other seasonings, such as herbs and spices, may be added at the beginning.

Safety

Never operate the oven while empty because without food or drink to absorb the microwaves, they will bounce straight back to the magnetron and shorten its life span. Similarly, melting a small quantity of fat or heating a tiny amount of liquid will have the same effect. It is therefore best to place a cup or tumbler of water in the oven at the same time.

Just in case an empty oven is switched on by accident, it is a wise safety measure to keep a container of water inside until the oven is required.

Cleaning

A wipe over with a damp cloth immediately after use will ensure that your microwave stays spotless and fresh.

If it does need cleaning, dampen a dish cloth and heat it for 30 to 45 seconds at defrost setting. Wipe over the top, base and sides of the oven then dry with a clean cloth.

To freshen the oven, put about 300 ml/½ pt/1¼ cups of water in a bowl in the oven and add a slice or two of fresh lemon. Heat on full power for 3 minutes or until the water is boiling and the oven steams up. Wipe the interior clean with a dish cloth then dry with a clean tea towel.

Controls and Settings

Microwave ovens vary in output, but most are about 600-700 watts. The wattage output controls the cooking time.

The recipes in this book use full power, which is 100 per cent power (600 watts) and medium power, which is 75 per cent power (450 watts). If your oven has a different output, the following guide may prove useful.

For a 500-watt oven, *increase* cooking time by about 20 per cent.

For a 550-watt oven, *increase* cooking time by about 10 per cent.

For a 650-watt oven, *decrease* cooking time by about 10 per cent.

For a 700-watt oven, *decrease* cooking time by about 20 per cent.

Using these figures will give a fairly accurate conversion time, but for greater accuracy, refer to your own microwave oven recipe books.

Variable Settings

If you have a microwave oven with variable power settings, you should follow the instructions in your own microwave guide book as all models vary and you will get the best results by following the guidelines specifically designed for your oven.

Notes on Recipes

1 Follow one set of measurements only, do not mix metric and Imperial.
2 Eggs are size 2.
3 Wash fresh produce before preparation.
4 Spoon measurements are level.
5 Adjust seasoning and strongly-flavoured ingredients, such as onions and garlic, to suit your own taste.
6 If you substitute dried for fresh herbs, use only half the amount specified.
7 Kcals are approximate.
8 Preparation times include both preparation and cooking and are approximate.

Microwave Cookware

Metal containers reflect microwaves away from the food and prevent it from cooking. Therefore you should never use metal containers or tins of any sort in the oven. It is also important to note that crockery with metal trims and manufacturers' names or pattern designs printed in gold or silver underneath could cause arcing in the microwave. This resembles tiny flashes of lightning. The arcing not only damages the magnetron but also ruins the metallic decoration.

The exceptions here are small amounts of foil used to cover poultry wing tips and ends of legs to prevent scorching. Also metal skewers for kebabs can be used if they are well covered by food. However, you must ensure that the skewers do not come into contact with any part of the oven interior. For complete safety, it is better to use wooden skewers.

Shallow dishes are better than deep ones for most recipes, except those used for some cakes and puddings which need headroom in order to rise satisfactorily. Round dishes give the best results, followed by oval. Sometimes food in rectangular or square dishes cook unevenly, especially at the corners.

In order for the microwaves to reach the food and cook it, the dishes chosen should be made of materials through which the microwaves can pass easily – like the sun's rays through a window pane. These are listed below.

Most suitable containers stay cool or even cold during cooking, but some kinds absorb heat from the cooked food and therefore become quite hot. For comfort and safety, therefore, you should always remove food from the oven using oven gloves.

Baskets
These may be used for brief reheating of rolls, for example. Prolonged use

n the microwave will cause them to dry out.

Glass
Pyrex-type glassware and ceramic glass are ideal for the microwave. Other sturdy glass may be used, but do not use good quality, fine glassware.

Paper
Kitchen paper or serviettes may be used to line the turntable if food is to be cooked directly on it, and it may also be used to cover food to prevent spluttering.

Microwave Plastic Wrap
Do not use ordinary clingfilm in a microwave oven. Select a film which specifically states that it is suitable for use in a microwave. To prevent the film from ballooning up in the oven and bursting, or being sucked back on to the food, puncture the film with a small slit made with the tip of a knife to allow the steam to escape.

Plastic
There is a whole range of rigid plastic containers available which are made specifically for use in the microwave. Most sturdy plastics are fine, but do not use yoghurt or cottage cheese containers or similar plastics! Plastic spatulas are useful as they can be left in a sauce while it is cooking and then used for stirring as and when required.

Pottery and Porcelain
Both of these can be used in the microwaves, although it is best to avoid high quality tea or dinner services. Avoid dark utensils as they become very hot.

Roasting Bags
These are ideal for cooking joints of meat or poultry. Make sure you close the tops with plastic bands or string, not metal ties.

Waxed Paper Products

These can only be used very briefly in the microwave otherwise the wax will begin to melt.

Wood
Wood, like basketware, dries out in the microwave and should be used only for brief reheating.

Browning Dish
This is a white ceramic dish, the base of which is coated with a special tin oxide material. It is preheated in the microwave so that the base becomes very hot and can sear food prior to cooking to give it a brown finish. Follow the manufacturer's instructions on preheating times, but it is usually about 6 minutes for steaks and chops, 2 minutes for eggs.

Temperature Probe
Some microwave ovens are fitted with a temperature probe like a thick knitting needle attached to a plastic-coated lead. One end slots into the oven while the other end is inserted into the food to be cooked and registers the internal temperature. The cooking cycle is therefore geared to temperature and not time and when the food registers the relevant temperature, the oven will switch off. Always follow the manufacturer's instructions.

Thawing

The microwave is very useful for thawing all kinds of things from meats to ready-meals. Always use the 'defrost' setting, cover the food and check it regularly, separating foods such as sausages as they begin to thaw. Remember that you often need to allow standing times while thawing, otherwise the outside of the food may begin to heat up while the inside is still frozen. For liquids, stir them occasionally while thawing.

Here are some thawing times for foods and ready-made dishes which you are most likely to have in your freezer. Check them against the manufacturer's instructions for your particular microwave.

Bacon: 3 mins, stand 6 mins.
Beefburgers(2 × 50 g/2 oz): 2 mins, stand 30 secs.
Bread (1 slice): 25 secs, stand 1 min.
(small loaf): 4 mins, stand 5 mins.
(large loaf): 7 mins, stand 8 mins.
(2 rolls): 1 min, stand 1 min.
Butter (225 g/8 oz/1 cup): 30 secs, stand 30 secs, 15 secs, stand 30 secs.
Cakes (individual): 45 secs, stand 3 mins.
(20 cm/8 in): 1½ mins, stand 2 mins.

Cannelloni (400 g/14 oz): 7 mins, stand 4 mins.
Chicken (whole): 10 mins, stand 20 mins, 5 mins, stand 10 mins.
(225 g/8 oz): 4 mins, stand 5 mins.
(225 g/8 oz cooked): 4 mins, stand 4 mins.
Chops (2 lamb or pork): 2 mins, stand 2 mins.

Cottage pie (individual): 3 mins, stand 2 mins.
Cream (300 ml/½ pt/1¼ cups): 1½ mins, stand 5 mins, 30 secs, stand 2 mins, repeat until thawed.
Duck (whole): 10 mins stand 30 mins, 6 mins, stand 15 mins.
Faggots (450 g/14 oz): 3 mins, stand 3 mins.

Fish (450 g/1 lb): 5 mins.
Fish in sauce (individual): 4 mins, stand 2 mins.
Fish, smoked (225 g/8 oz to serve cold): $2^1/_2$ mins, stand 3 mins.
Fruit juice (150 ml/$^1/_4$ pt/$^2/_3$ cup): 3 mins.
Ice cream (1 l/$1^3/_4$ pt/$4^1/_4$ cups to soften): 30 secs.

Lasagne (400 g/14 oz): 8 mins, stand 4 mins.
Liver (225 g/8 oz): 2 mins, stand 5 mins.
Meat (1.5 kg/3 lb joint): 10 mins, stand 20 mins, 5 mins, stand 20 mins.
Minced beef (225 g/8 oz): $1^1/_2$ mins, stand 5 mins, 1 $^1/_2$ mins, stand 5 mins.

Moussaka (400 g/14 oz): 7 mins, stand 4 mins.
Mousse (individual, to soften): 30 secs, stand 15 mins.
Pancakes (4 filled): 5 mins.
Pastry (400 g/14 oz): 2 mins.
Pâté (100 g/4 oz): 3 mins, stand 5 mins.
Pizza (225 g/8 oz): 3 mins, stand 2 mins.
Plated meal (individual): 4 mins, stand 3 mins.
Pork pies (individual): 2 mins, stand 15 mins.
Salmon, smoked (225 g/ 8 oz): 45 secs, stand 25 mins.
Sausages (450 g/1 lb large): 5 mins, stand 4 mins.
(450 g/1 lb chipolatas): 5 mins, stand 3 mins.
Sausagemeat (450 g/ 1 lb): $2^1/_2$ mins, stand 10 mins, $2^1/_2$ mins.
Sausage rolls (12 cooked): 4 mins, stand 4 mins.
Trifle (individual): 1 min, stand 5 mins.

Tricks of the Trade

Roast joints in a dish, with vegetables if liked. Cover and cook at full power for 7 minutes per 450 g/1 lb. Leave large joints to stand for 5 minutes at the middle and end of cooking, and small joints for 5 minutes at the end.

More sophisticated ovens may have a temperature probe or thermometer and gear cooking cycles to temperature rather than time. Refer to your manufacturer's instructions.

Arrange fish in a shallow dish, brush with melted butter, sprinkle with spices and a little salt, cover and cook for about 12 minutes per 450 g/1 lb on a low setting.

Cut all vegetables into similar walnut-sized pieces. Add just a small amount of liquid, cover and cook according to quantity and type.

Whole potatoes or pieces of potato should all be the same size. Put them into a dish with a little water, a pinch of salt and a knob of butter, cover and cook.

If you are warming a jar of food, use a temperature probe to prevent over-heating. It is better to re-heat baby food in a dish, stir thoroughly and test the food yourself before serving.

Special lids are available to cover plated meals for reheating. An inverted plate or shallow glass pie dish make excellent alternatives.

When buying cookware for the microwave, avoid square or rectangular shapes as foods in the corners tends to be over-cooked. Round or oval shapes are best.

Never use metal con-tainers in the microwave, or crockery with decora-tive metal trim as they will cause arcing and damage the decoration, and possibly the micro-wave oven as well.

If you are warming several plated meals at the same time, make sure you ar-range them in a circle around the outside of the turntable so that they heat up evenly.

A browning dish is useful to seal and brown foods which are then cooked in a sauce. This gives them more of the appearance of being cooked conventionally.

A deep cover is useful to prevent food which is being defrosted from dry-ing out.

Basic Cooking and Reheating Times

This handy chart will provide you with an easy reference to reheating frozen foods and cooking fresh foods in your microwave. Remember to choose a suitable-sized container and arrange the food in a single layer with the thickest parts at the outside. Cover with kitchen paper, microwave film, slit once or twice, or a roasting bag.

Always read the manufacturer's instructions for your own model and familiarise yourself with the controls as ovens do vary. It is better to undercook rather than overcook, as you can always return the food to the oven for a little longer but a few seconds too long can spoil some dishes.

Food	Cook on full power	Guidelines
Bacon rashers (225 g/8 oz)	3 mins, turn, 2 mins	Arrange in single layer on plate. Cover with kitchen paper. Drain after cooking.
Beefburgers (2 × 50 g/8oz)	1½ mins	Arrange in single layer on plate. Cover with kitchen paper. Drain after cooking.
Cannelloni (400 g/14 oz)	6 mins to reheat	Remove from foil container and place in dish. Cover with film.
Carrots (225 g/8 oz sliced)	10 mins	Add 30 ml/2 tbsp water. Cover with film.
Cauliflower florets (225 g/8 oz)	5 mins	Add 30 ml/2 tbsp water. Cover.
Chicken (whole or portions)	8 mins per 450 g/1 lb	Cook in roasting bag. Reposition during cooking. Stand 20 mins before carving.
Chicken (225 g/8 oz cooked)	3 mins, stand 3 mins	Arrange in single layer on plate. Cover with kitchen paper. Reposition during cooking.
Chops (225 g/8 oz)	4 mins	Arrange in single layer on plate. Cover with kitchen paper. Reposition during cooking.
Christmas pudding (individual)	45 secs, stand 1 min	Stand on plate. Cover with kitchen paper.
(450 g/1 lb)	3 mins, stand 2 mins	As above.
(900g/2 lb)	5 mins, stand 5 mins	As above.
Cottage pie (individual)	3 mins to reheat	Remove from foil container and place in dish. Cover with film.

Food	Cook on full power	Guidelines
Duck (whole or portions)	9 mins per 450 g/1 lb	Cook in roasting bag. Reposition during cooking. Stand 20 mins before carving.
Faggots (400 g/14 oz)	5 mins	Remove from foil container and place in dish. Cover with film.
Fish (450 g/1 lb)	8 mins	Top with knob of butter. Season after cooking.
Fish in sauce (individual)	3 mins to reheat	Snip bag before cooking.
Lasagne (400 g/14 oz)	6 mins to reheat	Remove from foil container and place in dish. Cover with film.
Meat (joints)	8 mins per 450 g/1 lb	Bone and roll joints for even cooking. Cook in roasting bag. Reposition during cooking. Stand 20 mins before carving.
Moussaka (400 g/14 oz)	6 mins to reheat	Remove from foil container and place in dish. Cover with film.
Pancakes (4 filled)	2 mins to reheat	Arrange on plate. Cover with kitchen paper.
Peas (450 g/1 lb)	6 mins	Add 30 ml/2 tbsp water. Cover.
Pizza (225 g/8 oz)	2 mins	Snip wrapping before cooking.
Plated meal (individual)	3 mins to reheat	Cover with film.
Potatoes (1 large jacket) (4 large jacket)	5 mins, stand 5 mins 12 mins, stand 5 mins	Prick with fork. Wrap in kitchen paper. Wrap in foil for standing. As above.
(450 g/1 lb)	5 mins	Add 60 ml/4 tbsp water. Cover.
Sausages (450 g/1 lb)	8 mins	Arrange on kitchen paper on plate. Cover with kitchen paper.

Starters

If you like to serve hot
starters but find it too
complicated with
conventional cooking, the
microwave can come to
your rescue as you can
prepare delicious starters
quickly and easily and
often serve them straight
from the oven.

*Stuffed Mushrooms,
page 18*

Stuffed Mushrooms

Serves 4
Preparation time: 20 mins
2200 kcal/9020 kJ

8 very large mushrooms
1 onion, chopped
400 g/*14 oz*/ minced pork
10 ml/*2 tsp* mild prepared mustard
10 ml/*2 tsp* green peppercorns
salt and freshly ground black pepper
5 ml/*1 tsp* paprika
5 ml/*1 tsp* curry powder
bunch parsley
30 ml/*2 tbsp* brandy
40 g/1 *1/2 oz*/3 tbsp butter or margarine
100 g/*4 oz* Emmental cheese, grated
a few lettuce leaves
1 box cress

1 Remove the stalks from the mushrooms and cut the stalks into slices. Mix with the onion, mince, mustard, peppercorns, seasoning and half the chopped parsley, then flavour with the brandy. Use to fill the mushroom caps.
2 Put the butter or margarine into a browning dish and heat on full power for 2 minutes.
3 Add the mushrooms, cover and cook on medium for 5 minutes.
4 Sprinkle the cheese on top, cover and cook on full power for 3 minutes.
5 Arrange the mushrooms on the lettuce leaves and garnish with the cress and remaining parsley.

Photograph page 16

Chicory Rolls

Serves 4
Preparation time: 25 mins
2160 kcal/8855 kJ

4 medium heads of chicory
8 slices boiled ham
10 ml/*2 tsp* tomato purée
10 ml/*2 tsp* mild prepared mustard
10 ml/*2 tsp* honey
10 ml/*2 tsp* green peppercorns, crushed
1 bunch chives, chopped
25 g/*1 oz*/2 tbsp butter or margarine
1 onion, chopped
100 g/ *4 oz* mushrooms, sliced
250 ml/8 fl *oz*/1 cup white wine
150 ml/ *1/4* pt/*2/3* cup single cream
salt and freshly ground black pepper
50 g/*2 oz* Parmesan cheese, grated
a pinch of nutmeg
a pinch of mixed spice
10 ml/*2 tsp* cornflour
10 ml/*2 tsp* water
8 slices Gouda cheese

1 Halve the chicory heads lengthwise, wash under running water and drain well. Place the ham slices on a work surface. Mix the tomato purée with the mustard, honey, crushed peppercorns and chives and spread on to the ham. Place a chicory half on each slice of ham, roll up and secure with a cocktail stick.
2 Place the butter or margarine in a browning dish and heat on full power for 2 minutes. Add the onion and mushrooms, cover and cook on full power for 2 minutes.
3 Add the chicory rolls. Mix wine, cream, salt and pepper, stir in the Parmesan and season with nutmeg. Pour on to the chicory, cover the dish and cook on medium for minutes.
4 Transfer the rolls to a dish. Season the sauce well with salt, pepper and mixed spice. Mix the cornflour with the water and blend it into the sauce. Replace the chicory and cover each one with a slice of Gouda. Cover and cook on full power for minutes. Stand for 2 minutes before serving.

Photograph opposite

Herb Celery Sticks

Serves 4
Preparation time: 30 mins
3840 kcal/15744 kJ

---

*100 g/**4 oz** ham, diced*

40 g/1 ¹/₂ oz/3 tbsp butter

1 bunch spring onions, cut into strips

*250 ml/**8 fl oz**/1 cup stock*

*250 ml/**8 fl oz**/1 cup white wine*

*400 g/**14 oz** celery sticks, cut into pieces*

salt and freshly ground white pepper

a pinch of nutmeg

2 tomatoes, skinned, deseeded and chopped

*150 ml/¹/₄ **pt**/²/₃ cup soured cream*

2 eggs

*200 g/**7 oz** Mozzarella cheese, cubed*

¹/₂ bunch parsley, chopped

¹/₂ bunch chervil, chopped

¹/₂ bunch chives, chopped

1 Place the ham and butter in a browning dish and cook on full power for 3 minutes. Add the spring onions, stock and wine. Arrange the celery on top and season with salt, pepper and nutmeg. Cover and cook on medium for 10 minutes.
2 Sprinkle on the tomatoes. Combine the remaining ingredients and spoon over the surface. Cover and cook on full power for 5 minutes.

Photograph (left)

Courgette Boats

Serves 4
Preparation time: 30 mins
2460 kcal/10085 kJ

450 g/1 *lb* sausage meat
2 onions, chopped
2 eggs
1 bread roll, soaked until soft in cold water
salt and freshly ground black pepper
5 ml/1 *tsp* basil
5 ml/1 *tsp* oregano
1 bunch parsley, chopped
2 medium-sized courgettes
2 cloves garlic, chopped
30 ml/2 *tbsp* olive oil
150 ml/¹/₄ *pt*/²/₃ cup stock
200 g/7 *oz* canned tomatoes
a pinch of mixed spice
5 ml/1 *tsp* grated lemon rind
100 g/4 *oz* Parmesan cheese, grated

1 Mix the sausage meat with 1 onion, the eggs, squeezed bread roll, salt, pepper, basil, oregano and parsley. Halve the courgettes, remove the seeds and fill with meat.
2 Cook the oil, garlic and remaining onions on full power until soft. Add the stock, tomatoes with their juice, mixed spice and lemon rind. Arrange the courgettes and spoon some of the juice over them. Sprinkle with half the Parmesan and cook on medium for 15 minutes. Sprinkle with Parmesan.

Photograph (right)

21

Salami Toasts

Serves 4
Preparation time: 20 mins
3240 kcal/13275 kJ

4 slices wholemeal bread

45 ml/**3 tbsp** horseradish sauce

12 slices German ham sausage

12 slices salami

4 large tomatoes, skinned and sliced

salt and freshly ground black pepper

5 ml/**1 tsp** oregano

5 ml/**1 tsp** basil

40 g/1 1/2 **oz**/3 tbsp butter or margarine

2 onions, cut into rings

1 red pepper, cut into strips

8 slices processed cheese

1 bunch radishes, sliced

1 bunch chives, chopped

1 Toast the bread then spread it with horseradish sauce. Place 3 slices of ham sausage and salami on to each and arrange the tomatoes on top. Sprinkle with salt, pepper, oregano and basil.
2 Heat the butter or margarine in a browning dish on full power for 2 minutes. Add the onions and pepper, cover and cook on full power for 3 minutes. Remove from the dish and spread evenly on top of the ham and sausage toasts. Top each one with 2 slices of cheese. Arrange on a large plate.

3 Cook on full power for 5 to 7 minutes. Transfer to individual plates then decorate with radishes and chives before serving.

Photograph opposite (top)

Gourmet Tip
You can vary the ingredients as much as you like. Try different cold meats, prawns, spring onions or gherkins.

Luxury Salad Toasts

Serves 4
Preparation time: 25 mins
3880 kcal/15910 kJ

50 g/**2 oz**/¹/₄ cup butter or margarine

15 ml/**1 tbsp** chopped fresh parsley

4 medium-sized naan or pitta breads

150 ml/¹/₄ **pt**/²/₃ cup soured cream

225 g/**8 oz** Emmental cheese, grated

2 eggs

salt and freshly ground black pepper

¹/₂ cucumber, sliced

2 tomatoes, sliced

1 courgette, sliced

100 g/**4 oz** boiled ham, diced

100 g/**4 oz** salami, diced

4 large gherkins, diced

4 slices processed cheese

tomato ketchup to taste

30 ml/**2 tbsp** chopped fresh chives

1 Mix together the butter or margarine and parsley and spread it on the bread. Whisk the soured cream with half the Emmental cheese, the eggs, and salt and pepper to taste. Put equal amounts on to the breads.
2 Divide the sliced vegetables on top of cheese mixture. Season. Mix the diced ingredients with the remaining Emmental and arrange on the vegetable slices. Place a slice of processed cheese on top. Cover and cook individually on full power for 2 to 3 minutes.
3 Serve garnished with tomato ketchup and chives.

Photograph opposite (bottom)

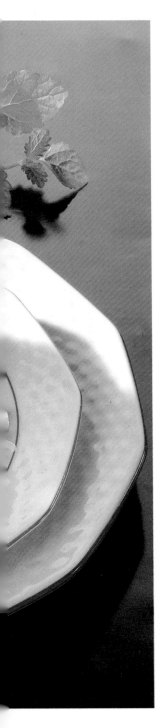

Prawn Ragout
Vol-au-Vent

Serves 4
Preparation time: 30 mins
3520 kcal/14430 kJ

---

40 g/1 ¹/₂ oz/3 tbsp butter or margarine

1 bunch spring onions, sliced

100 g/4 oz boiled ham, diced

100 g/4 oz oyster mushrooms, chopped

2 slices pineapple, diced

450 g/1 lb peeled prawns

5 ml/1 tsp green peppercorns

juice of 1 lemon

juice of 1 orange

150 ml/¹/₄ pt/²/₃ cup white wine

150 ml/¹/₄ pt/²/₃ cup crème fraîche

150 ml/¹/₄ pt/²/₃ cup meat stock

10 ml/2 tsp cornflour

salt and freshly ground black pepper

a pinch of nutmeg

a few drops of Worcestershire sauce

1 bunch dill, chopped

8 puff pastry vol-au-vent cases

1 Put the butter or margarine into a heat resistant glass or porcelain dish and heat on full power for 2 minutes. Add the oyster mushrooms, spring onions and ham. Cover and cook on full power for 3 minutes.

2 Add the pineapple and prawns, stir in the peppercorns, then add the lemon and orange juices with the wine. Combine the crème fraîche smoothly with the stock and cornflour, add to the prawns and season well with salt, pepper, nutmeg and Worcestershire sauce. Cover and cook on full power for 5 minutes. Remove and season again. Fold in the dill. Keep hot.

3 Cover and heat up the puff pastry vol-au-vent cases on full power for 3 minutes. Spoon the prawn ragout into each one and garnish with dill. Serve hot.

Mussel Pots

Serves 4
Preparation time: 25 mins
2280 kcal/9350 kJ

---

450 g/1 *lb* shelled mussels

salt and freshly ground black pepper

juice of 1 lemon

a few drops of Worcestershire sauce

1 bunch spring onions, sliced

4 tomatoes, skinned

100 g/4 *oz* mushrooms, chopped

225 g/8 *oz*/1 cup butter or margarine, softened

2 garlic cloves, chopped

4 anchovy fillets, chopped

1/2 bunch tarragon, chopped

1/2 bunch chervil, chopped

1/2 bunch parsley, chopped

1/2 bunch dill, chopped

15 ml/1 *tbsp* mild mustard

---

1 Place the mussels in a bowl, season with salt and pepper then add the lemon juice and Worcestershire sauce. Mix in the vegetables and leave for 1 hour in the refrigerator to marinate.
2 Meanwhile, beat the butter or margarine until creamy then add the garlic, anchovies, herbs and mustard and mix well.
3 Divide the mussels between individual dishes and add equal amounts of herb butter to each. Cover and cook on full power for 3 to 4 minutes.

Photograph opposite (centre)

Multi-Coloured Pancakes

Serves 4
Preparation time: 40 mins
2600 kcal/10660 kJ

---

8 potato pancakes (see Gourmet Tip)

200 g/7 *oz* medium-fat curd cheese

15 ml/1 *tbsp* cranberry sauce

salt and freshly ground black pepper

a pinch of chilli pepper

15 ml/1 *tbsp* brandy

100 g/4 *oz* lean bacon, cut into strips

1 onion, chopped

225 g/8 *oz* mixed vegetables

2 slices pineapple, diced

a pinch of nutmeg

45 ml/3 *tbsp* crème fraîche seasoned with chopped herbs

1 box cress

---

1 Mix together the cheese and cranberry sauce until smooth. Season well with salt, pepper and chilli pepper and flavour with brandy. Spread over the pancakes and put each one on to a plate.
2 Place the bacon in a browning dish and cook on full power for 3 minutes. Add the onion and mixed vegetables, cover and cook on full power for 5 to 8 minutes.
3 Add the pineapple. Season with nutmeg and extra salt and pepper. Spoon the vegetable mixture on the pancakes, cover and warm each pancake on full power for 2 to 3 minutes.
4 Remove and dot with a dab of crème fraîche then sprinkle with cress and serve.

Photograph opposite (top and bottom)

Gourmet Tip
To make potato pancakes, mix 450 g/1 lb grated potato, 1 grated onion, 30 ml/2 tbsp plain flour, 2 eggs, salt and pepper. Heat a little oil and fry until crisp and golden on both sides.

One-Pot Cooking

If there were such a thing as a top-ten chart for ways of preparation, then these dishes would come close to number one. Whether it is a soup, vegetable-mix, stew or minced meat, all your favourite one-pot dishes can be successfully prepared in the microwave.

Gardener's Soup, page 30

Gardener's Soup

Serves 4
Preparation time: 30 mins
1860 kcal/7625 kJ

25 g/**1** *oz*/2 tbsp butter or margarine

100 g/**4** *oz* boiled ham, diced

100 g/**4** *oz* German sausage, sliced

100 g/**4** *oz* cauliflower florets

100 g/**4** *oz* broccoli florets

100 g/**4** *oz* carrots, sliced

100 g/**4** *oz* peas

100 g/**4** *oz* asparagus tips

375 ml/**13 fl** *oz*/1 ½ cups meat stock

150 ml/**¼** *pt*/²⁄₃cup single cream

10 ml/**2 tsp** cornflour

a few drops of Worcestershire sauce

juice of ½ lemon

salt and freshly ground black pepper

a pinch of nutmeg

½ bunch chervil, chopped

½ bunch chives, chopped

1 Place the butter or margarine in large heat-resistant glass or porcelain dish. Add the ham, cover and cook on full power for 2 minutes. Mix in the sausage, cover and cook on full power for a further 2 minutes.
2 Add the cauliflower, broccoli, carrots, peas and asparagus. Pour on the stock. Blend the cream smoothly with the cornflour and stir into the vegetables.

3 Season well with the Worcestershire sauce, lemon juice, salt, pepper and nutmeg. Cover and cook on medium for 12 to 14 minutes.
4 Remove from the oven, season again, sprinkle with the herbs and serve.

Photograph page 28

Gourmet Tip
Make sure you use vegetables with similar cooking times and cut them into similar-sized pieces. Deep-frozen food will have been blanched in advance so the cooking times of the various types of vegetables should be more or less the same and may therefore be mixed and cooked together.

Fish Stew

Serves 4
Preparation time: 30 mins
1720 kcal/7050 kJ

25 g/**1** *oz*/2 tbsp butter or margarine

1 onion, chopped

2 carrots, diced

1 bunch celery, diced

150 ml/**¼** *pt*/²⁄₃ cup light white wine

400 g/**14** *oz* cod fillet, skinned

10 ml/**2 tsp** cornflour

75 ml/**5 tbsp** single cream

375 ml/**13 fl** *oz*/1½ cups meat stock

salt and freshly ground black pepper

a few drops of Worcestershire sauce

a pinch of sugar

1 bunch dill, chopped

300 ml/½ *pt*/1¼ cups whipping cream, lightly whipped

2 egg yolks

1 Place the butter or margarine in a heat-resistant dish and heat on full power for 2 minutes. Add the vegetables and wine cover and cook on full power for 5 minutes Stand for 3 minutes Uncover.
2 Cut the fish into walnut sized pieces and add to the vegetables. Stir the cornflour into the cream and pour into the dish with meat stock. Cover and cook on full power for 8 to 10 minutes. Season with salt, pepper, Worcestershire sauce and sugar.
3 Stir in the dill. Mix the egg yolks with the whipped cream and carefully fold into the soup. Cover and cook on full power for 1 minute.

Photograph opposite

31

Chervil Soup

Serves 4
Preparation time: 35 mins
2280 kcal/9350 kJ

40 g/1 ½ oz/3 tbsp butter or margarine
1 onion, chopped
200 g/7 oz potatoes, diced
25 g/1 oz celery, diced
1 leek, diced
250 ml/8 fl oz/1 cup white wine
375 ml/13 fl oz/1 ½ cups meat stock
1 bunch chervil, chopped
500 ml/17 fl oz/2 ¼ cups single cream
salt and freshly ground black pepper
10 ml/2 tsp cornflour
a pinch of sugar
a pinch of nutmeg
225 g/8 oz smoked salmon, cut into strips
2 egg yolks
a few sprigs of chervil

1 Cook the butter or margarine, vegetables and wine, covered, on full power for 10 minutes. Purée with the stock and chervil.
2 Heat up the purée with 75 ml/5 tbsp of cream on defrost. Season with salt, pepper, sugar and nutmeg. Mix the cornflour with a little cream and stir it in. Fold in the salmon strips, remaining cream and egg yolks.
3 Cook on full power for 4 minutes. Serve garnished with chervil.

Photograph (top)

Tomato Soup

Serves 4
Preparation time: 25 mins
2020 kcal/8280 kJ

---

25 g/*1 oz*/2 tbsp butter or margarine
5 ml/*1 tsp* salt
1 clove garlic
2 onions, chopped
800 g/1³/₄ *lb* tomatoes, skinned and diced
250 ml/*8 fl oz*/1 cup white wine
250 ml/*8 fl oz*/1 cup stock
150 ml/¹/₄ *pt*/²/₃ cup crème fraîche
10 ml/*2 tsp* cornflour
salt and freshly ground black pepper
a pinch of sugar
200 g/*7 oz* prawns, peeled
30 ml/*2 tbsp* gin
450 ml/³/₄ *pt*/2¹/₄ cups double cream, whipped

1 Heat the butter or margarine on full power for 2 minutes. Crush the garlic with salt and add to the dish with the onions. Cover and cook on full power for 2 minutes. Add the tomatoes and wine and cook on full power for 6 minutes.
2 Purée in a mixer, transfer to a deep bowl and add the stock. Mix the crème fraîche with the cornflour and stir into the soup. Season, add the prawns, cover and cook on full power for 5 minutes.
3 Flavour with gin, fold in the cream and serve.

Photograph (bottom)

Sausage Hot-Pot

Serves 4
Preparation time: 35 mins
3040 kcal/12465 kJ

---

30 ml/*2 tbsp* olive oil

1 bunch spring onions, chopped

1 red pepper, diced

200 g/*7 oz* potatoes, diced

150 ml/*¹/₄ pt/²/₃ cup* tomato ketchup

5 ml/*1 tsp* mild curry paste

300 ml/*¹/₂ pt/1 ¹/₄ cups* tomato juice

5 ml/*1 tsp* thyme

5 ml/*1 tsp* marjoram

2 garlic cloves, crushed

2 Frankfurter sausages, sliced

100 g/*4 oz* Italian Salami, diced

6 pork sausages, sliced

250 ml/*8 fl oz/1 cup* meat stock

400 g/*14 oz* canned red kidney beans

salt and freshly ground black pepper

a pinch of mixed spice

a few drops of vinegar

a pinch of sugar

a few drops of tabasco sauce

---

1 Place the oil in a heat-resistant glass or porcelain dish. Add the vegetables, ketchup, curry paste, tomato juice, herbs, garlic, and the Frankfurters, Salami and pork sausages. Fill up with stock then add the beans and remaining ingredients. Cover and cook on medium for 12 to 14 minutes. Stand for 5 minutes. Stir well.
2 Continue to cook on full power for 5 minutes.

Photograph opposite (top)

Vegetable Tureen

Serves 4
Preparation time: 40 mins
1840 kcal/7545 kJ

---

20 ml/*4 tsp* olive oil

100 g/*4 oz* smoked streaky bacon, diced

2 chicken breast fillets, diced

2 onions, chopped

2 carrots, sliced

1 small head savoy cabbage

500 ml/*17 fl oz/2¹/₄ cups* meat stock

5 ml/*1 tsp* caraway seeds

a pinch of nutmeg

salt and freshly ground black pepper

a few drops of Worcestershire sauce

200 g/*7 oz* canned peas

200 g/*7 oz* canned butter beans

a pinch of mixed spice

150 ml/*¹/₄ pt/²/₃ cup* soured cream

30 ml/*2 tbsp* chopped fresh chives

---

1 Place the oil and diced bacon in a heat-resistant glass dish. Cover and cook on full power for minutes. Add the chicken cover and cook on full power for a further minutes.
2 Add the onions and carrots. Clean the savoy cabbage, halve, remove the stalk and cut the leaves into strips 1 cm/¹ in wide. Add the vegetables to the meat, pour over the meat stock then season with caraway seeds, nutmeg, salt, pepper and Worcestershire sauce. Cover and cook on full power for 10 minutes.
3 Add the peas and the beans to the vegetables season well again with mixed spice, cover and cook on full power for further 5 minutes.
4 Remove from the oven fold in the soured cream and serve sprinkled with chives.

Photograph opposite (bottom)

Gourmet Tip
There is a more savoury variation to the vegetable tureen. Use cold roast pork instead of chicken breast, and sauerkraut instead of savoy cabbage.

Seafood Spectacular

Serves 4
Preparation time: 35 mins
1660 kcal/6805 kJ

---

30 ml/*2 tbsp* olive oil

1 onion, chopped

2 carrots, diced

1 small head of celery, coarsely chopped

1 red pepper, cut into strips

1 green pepper, cut into strips

1 small courgette, sliced

250 ml/*8 fl oz*/1 cup rosé wine

1 bay leaf

3 cloves

4 juniper berries

375 ml/*13 fl oz*/1¹/₂ cups fish or meat stock

400 g/*14 oz* canned tomatoes

100 g/*4 oz* squid rings

200 g/*7 oz* lemon sole fillet, cut into chunks

100 g/*4 oz* cooked mussels, shelled

4 cooked Dublin Bay prawns

50 g/*2 oz*/¹/₂ cup walnut halves

50 g/*2 oz*/¹/₃ cup sultanas

a dash of Madeira

salt and freshly ground black pepper

juice of 1 lemon

a pinch of sugar

30 ml/*2 tbsp* chopped fresh basil

1 Pour the oil into a heat-resistant glass or porcelain dish and heat on full power for 2 minutes. Add the vegetables, cover and cook on full power for 5 minutes. Pour on the wine, add the bay leaf, cloves and juniper berries, cover and cook for a further 5 minutes.
2 Add the stock, tomatoes, squid rings, the sole, mussels and prawns. Cover and cook on full power for 10 to 12 minutes.
3 Stir in the walnut halves, sultanas and Madeira. Season well with salt, pepper, lemon juice and sugar.
4 Cover and cook on full power for 3 to 5 minutes, sprinkle with basil and serve.

Pickled Cabbage Goulash

Serves 4
Preparation time: 45 mins
2600 kcal/10660 kJ

---

30 ml/*2 tbsp* lard

450 g/*1 lb* stewing pork, cubed

salt and freshly ground black pepper

10 ml/*2 tsp* paprika

4 onions, sliced

1 red pepper, cut into strips

1 green pepper, cut into strips

20 ml/*4 tsp* tomato purée

1 glass light ale

450 g/*1 lb* sauerkraut

450 ml/*³/₄ pt*/2 cups meat stock

20 ml/*4 tsp* honey

10 ml/*2 tsp* caraway seeds

10 ml/*2 tsp* marjoram

1 bay leaf

4 juniper berries

75 ml/*5 tbsp* crème fraîche

---

1 Heat the lard in a flameproof glass or porcelain dish on a conventional cooker. Season the meat well with pepper, salt and paprika, then brown it in the lard. Add the vegetables and cool until slightly softened.
2 Fold in the tomato purée and pour on the ale. Separate the sauerkraut and add with the meat stock. Season with honey, caraway seeds, marjoram, bay leaf and juniper berries. Cover and cook on medium for 15 minutes, stirring frequently.
3 Finally, season once more with salt and pepper and fold in the crème fraîche. Cover and cook on full power for 5 minutes, remove and serve.

Photograph opposite (top)

```
Gourmet Tip
Hollow out a firm
savoy cabbage to
use as a dish for this
recipe.
```

Vegetable and Pork Casserole

Serves 4
Preparation time: 40 mins
2380 kcal/9760 kJ

---

30 ml/*2 tbsp* olive oil

1 garlic clove, crushed

600 g/*1¹/₂ lb* pork fillet, sliced

salt and freshly ground black pepper

10 ml/*2 tsp* marjoram

10 ml/*2 tsp* grated lemon rind

1 onion, chopped

1 red pepper, diced

1 green pepper, diced

200 g/*7 oz* mixture of peas and carrots

250 ml/*8 fl oz*/1 cup white wine

250 ml/*8 fl oz*/1 cup stock

75 ml/*5 tbsp* crème fraîche

¹/₂ bunch chives, chopped

---

1 Heat the oil and garlic in a flameproof dish on a conventional cooker. Season the meat with salt and pepper, rub in the marjoram and lemon rind, add to the dish and fry in the oil until brown. Add the vegetables, cover with the wine then stir in the stock. Cover and cook on medium for 20 to 25 minutes.
2 Add the crème fraîche, cover and cook on full power for 5 minutes. Remove from the oven and fold in the chives.

Photograph opposite (bottom)

Main Courses

Don't restrict yourself to using the microwave only for reheating or simple basics. You can create some wonderful main courses to rival any conventionally cooked dish.

Pork and Sprout Hot-Pot, page 42

Pork and Sprout Hot-Pot

Serves 4
Preparation time: 40 mins
3360 kcal/13775 kJ

30 ml/2 tbsp butter or margarine

100 g/4 oz lean uncooked gammon, diced

400 g/14 oz minced pork

1 onion, chopped

1 small leek, diced

2 cloves garlic

5 ml/1 tsp salt

5 ml/1 tsp oregano

5 ml/1 tsp basil

400 g/14 oz canned tomatoes

250 ml/8 fl oz/1 cup white wine

salt and freshly ground black pepper

a pinch of mixed spice

450 g/1 lb sprouts

375 ml/13 fl oz/1 1/2 cups béchamel sauce

100 g/4 oz Emmental cheese, grated

1 Heat the butter or margarine in a frying pan on a conventional cooker. Add the gammon and the minced pork and brown. Mix in the onion and leek and simmer for 7 minutes. Crush the garlic with the salt. Add to the pan with the oregano, basil, tomatoes and white wine. Season with salt, pepper and mixed spice.

2 Place the sprouts in a dish with 30 ml/2 tbsp of water and microwave on full power for 5 minutes, until partially cooked.

3 Arrange the sprouts and meat mixture in alternate layers in a heat-resistant glass dish.

4 Mix together the béchamel sauce and Emmental cheese, pour over the top of sprouts then cover and cook on medium for 15 minutes.

Photograph page 40

Gourmet Tip
One of the best flavouring ingredients is garlic – from both the health and flavour viewpoints. Potent, yes, so a little goes a long way, but when crushed with salt, some of the volatile oils will evaporate and the flavour, as a result, becomes less intense.

Turkey in Piquant Sauce

Serves 4
Preparation time: 40 mins
2760 kcal/11315 kJ

30 ml/2 tbsp butter or margarine

600 g/1 1/4 lb turkey or hare fillet, cut into chunks

2 onions, sliced

1 red pepper, cut into strips

1 green pepper, cut into strips

100 g/4 oz sweetcorn

250 ml/8 fl oz/1 cup red wine

20 ml/4 tsp tomato purée

250 ml/8 fl oz/1 cup gravy

salt and freshly ground black pepper

10 ml/2 tsp marjoram

5 ml/1 tsp thyme

a few drops of Worcestershire sauce

a few drops of tabasco sauce

150 ml/1/4 pt/2/3 cup soured cream

1 Heat the butter or margarine in a browning dish on full power for 2 minutes. Add the turkey or hare, stir and cook on full power for 5 minutes.

2 Add the vegetables, wine, purée, gravy, spices and herbs. Cover and cook on medium for 10 minutes.

3 Season with Worcestershire and tabasco sauce, fold in the cream, cover and cook on full power for 3 minutes.

Photograph opposite

Cabbage Rolls

Serves 4
Preparation time: 45 mins
2420 kcal/9920 kJ

12 white cabbage leaves, blanched
200 g/*7 oz* ham, diced
6 mushrooms, diced
6 spring onions, chopped
100 g/*4 oz* Mozzarella cheese, diced
45 ml/*3 tbsp* breadcrumbs
2 eggs
1 bunch chives, chopped
15 ml/*1 tbsp* butter
1 glass sparkling wine
250 ml/*8 fl oz*/1 cup white sauce
juice of ¹/₂ lemon
75 ml/*5 tbsp* crème fraîche
a few drops of Worcestershire sauce
salt and pepper
10 ml/*2 tsp* cornflour
15 ml/*1 tbsp* cold water

1 For each roll, pile up three cabbage leaves. Mix the gammon, vegetables, cheese, breadcrumbs, eggs and chives and spread on the leaves. Shape into rolls and place in a greased dish with the butter. Cover and cook on full power for 5 minutes.
2 Add the wine, white sauce, lemon juice and crème fraîche. Cover and cook on medium for 15 minutes.
3 Season. Mix the cornflour and water and stir in. Cover and cook on full power for 4 minutes.

Photograph (top)

44

Beef Roulade in Campari Sauce

Serves 4
Preparation time: 50 mins
3580 kcal/14680 kJ

4 thin slices beef
salt and pepper
*20 ml/**4 tsp** mild mustard*
4 rashers lean bacon
*200 g/**7 oz** sausage meat*
1 gherkin, chopped
¹/₂ bunch parsley, chopped
*2.5 ml/¹/₂ **tsp** paprika*
*30 ml/**2 tbsp** breadcrumbs*
*30 ml/**2 tbsp** olive oil*
1 onion, sliced into rings
1 red pepper, cut into strips
*100 g/**4 oz** mushrooms, sliced*
*450 ml/³/₄ **pt**/2 cups Campari*
*450 ml/³/₄ **pt**/2 cups gravy*
*75 ml/**3 tbsp** crème fraîche*
*10 ml/**2 tsp** tabasco sauce*

1 Season the beef with salt and pepper, spread with mustard and top each slice with a bacon rasher. Knead the sausage meat, gherkin, herbs, paprika and breadcrumbs. Spread on the slices and roll up.
2 Heat the oil in a frying pan on a conventional cooker, add the rolls and lightly fry. Transfer to a heat-resistant dish. Add the vegetables, Campari, gravy, crème fraîche and tabasco sauce. Cover and cook on medium for 25 to 30 minutes.

Photograph (bottom)

Beef and Carrot Roast

Serves 4
Preparation time: 80 mins
3240 kcal/13285 kJ

1 kg/*2 lb* boneless joint of beef for roasting

salt and freshly ground black pepper

10 ml/*2 tsp* paprika

2 carrots, cut into slivers

fat for frying

1 onion, sliced

2 carrots, cut into strips

1 celery stick, cut into strips

1 leek, cut into strips

1 glass lager

200 g/*7 oz* canned tomatoes

250 ml/*8 fl oz*/1 cup gravy

30 ml/*2 tbsp* honey

30 ml/*2 tbsp* fruit vinegar

10 ml/*2 tsp* marjoram

5 ml/*1 tsp* thyme

1 Season the roast beef with salt, pepper and paprika. Thread the carrot slivers into the meat, using a larding needle or skewer. Heat the fat in a frying pan on a conventional cooker and brown the meat all over. Place in a heat-resistant dish, cover and cook on medium for 10 minutes.
2 Add the vegetables, pour in the lager, then add the tomatoes and gravy. Stir in the remaining ingredients, cover and cook on medium for 40 to 50 minutes.

3 Cut the meat into slices, coat with the sauce and serve.

Photograph opposite (top)

Breast of Pork with Vegetables

Serves 4
Preparation time: 65 mins
4280 kcal/17550 kJ

1 kg/*2 lb* pork fillet or turkey breast fillet

salt and freshly ground black pepper

10 ml/*2 tsp* marjoram

5 ml/*1 tsp* paprika

2 cloves garlic, crushed

10 ml/*2 tsp* grated lemon rind

250 g/*9 oz* sausage meat

45 ml/*3 tbsp* crème fraîche

2 eggs

30 ml/*2 tbsp* plain flour

1 bunch parsley, chopped

a pinch of nutmeg

fat for frying

250 ml/*8 fl oz*/1 cup red wine

450 ml/*³/4 pt*/2 cups meat stock

4 carrots, cut into strips

1 leek, cut into strips

8 small onions, peeled

1 small head celery, separated

5 ml/*1 tsp* thyme

a pinch of mixed spice

10 ml/*2 tsp* cornflour

15 ml/*1 tbsp* cold water

1 Using a sharp knife, cu a deep pocket in the porl or turkey breast fillet. Sea son both sides well witr salt, pepper, marjoram paprika, crushed garlic and lemon rind.
2 To make the filling, pu the sausage meat into a bowl. Add the crème fraîche, eggs, flour and parsley and work it into a compact mixture. Seasor well with salt, pepper and nutmeg. Put the filling inte the pocket, close witl skewers or sew shut with a needle and thread.
3 Melt the fat in a fryin pan on a conventiona cooker and brown th meat all over. Transfer it t a heat-resistant glass c porcelain dish with th meat juices. Add the win and stock. Arrange th vegetables around th meat, sprinkle with thyme cover and cook on me dium for 40 to 45 minutes
4 Remove the meat, sea son the sauce with mixe spice, salt and peppe Add the cornflou smoothly mixed with th water. Replace the mea cover and cook on ft power for 5 minutes. Re move the meat and c into slices. Coat with th sauce and serve.

Photograph opposite (bottom)

Steamed Trout with Vegetables

Serves 4
Preparation time: 30 mins
2080 kcal/8530 kJ

---

4 trout

salt and freshly ground black pepper

juice of 2 lemons

a few drops of Worcestershire sauce

1 bunch dill, chopped

1 bunch parsley, chopped

2 carrots, cut into narrow chips

1 bunch spring onions, cut into strips

1 large onion, cut into rings

100 g/4 oz mushrooms, sliced

1 lime or lemon, peeled and sliced

a pinch of nutmeg

1 bay leaf

4 juniper berries

250 ml/8 fl oz/1 cup white wine

375 ml/13 fl oz/2 cups meat stock

100 g/4 oz/¹/₂ cup butter, softened

30 ml/2 tbsp chopped parsley

---

1 Wash the trout under running water, dab dry then season with salt and pepper. Sprinkle with lemon juice and Worcestershire sauce and marinate for 10 minutes. Pack the dill and parsley inside each trout.

2 Arrange the trout in a capacious dish and scatter the vegetables on top. Arrange the lemon slices on top of the vegetables. Sprinkle lightly with nutmeg, add the bay leaf and the juniper berries then coat with the wine and stock. Mix the butter and parsley and dot all over the dish.

3 Cover and cook on medium for 15 to 20 minutes. Serve the trout with the vegetables and liquid from dish.

Cod in Savoy Cabbage

Serves 4
Preparation time: 40 mins
2620 kcal/10740 kJ

---

4 cod fillets, skinned

salt and freshly ground
black pepper

a few drops of
Worcestershire sauce

a few drops lemon juice

a few drops of white wine

12 savoy cabbage leaves,
blanched

4 slices boiled ham

4 slices fresh Gouda
cheese

200 g/*7 oz* peeled prawns

2 tomatoes, skinned,
deseeded and diced

45 ml/*3 tbsp* crème fraîche

1 bunch dill, chopped

30 ml/*2 tbsp* butter or
margarine

1 onion, cut into rings

1 bunch spring onions, cut
into strips

1 orange, in segments

250 ml/*8 fl oz*/1 cup white
wine

150 ml/*¹/₄ pt*/*²/₃* cup single
cream

a pinch of mixed spice

6 mint leaves, chopped

15 ml/*1 tbsp* orange liqueur

---

1 Season the cod with
salt and pepper, sprinkle
with Worcestershire
sauce, lemon juice and
wine and marinate for 15
to 20 minutes.
2 Place 2 to 3 cabbage
leaves, one on top of the
other, on a work surface.
Lay the cod fillets on top
then cover each with a
slice of ham topped with a
slice of Gouda.
3 Mix together the
prawns, tomatoes and
crème fraîche. Fold in the
dill, season well with salt
and pepper and spread
on top of the cheese.
Close the leaves tightly
around the fish and se-
cure with cocktail sticks or
tie with kitchen thread.
Place in a greased heat-
resistant glass or por-
celain dish. Cover and
cook on full power for 5
minutes.
4 Add the onion, spring
onions, orange, wine and
cream. Season with salt,
pepper and mixed spice.
Cover and cook on me-
dium for 12 to 15 minutes.
Adjust the seasoning, fold
in the mint, flavour with orange liqueur and serve.

*Photograph opposite
(top)*

Sole Roll-Ups with Mushrooms

Serves 4
Preparation time: 25 mins
1900 kcal/7790 kJ

---

8 sole fillets

salt and freshly ground
black pepper

juice of 1 lemon

a few drops of
Worcestershire sauce

30 ml/*2 tbsp* butter or
margarine

4 shallots, chopped

100 g/*4 oz* boiled ham,
diced

400 g/*14 oz* mushrooms,
chopped

250 ml/*8 fl oz*/1 cup meat
stock

150 ml/*¹/₄ pt*/*²/₃* cup single
cream

10 ml/*2 tsp* cornflour

15 ml/*1 tbsp* cold water

a pinch of saffron

a pinch of sugar

a dash of Martini Bianco

---

1 Season the fish with sa
and pepper and marinat
in the lemon juice an
Worcestershire sauce fo
at least 15 minutes. Ro
up and hold in place wit
cocktail sticks. Place in
heat-resistant dish.
2 Melt the butter or ma
garine in a frying pan on
conventional cooker, ac
the shallots and fry un
soft. Add the ham ar
mushrooms and fry lightl
Cover in the stock, ac
the cream and the cor
flour mixed smoothly wi
cold water. Season ar
flavour with saffron, sug
and Martini Bianco.
3 Arrange the mushroo
mixture on the rolls of sol
cover and cook on f
power for 10 minutes.

*Photograph opposite
(bottom)*

Lamb Ragout

Serves 4
Preparation time: 1 hour
2700 kcal/11070 kJ

*600 g/1 ¹/₂ **lb** lamb, diced*
salt and pepper
2 cloves garlic, crushed
*10 ml/**2 tsp** chopped mint*
*5 ml/**1 tsp** thyme*
*30 ml/**2 tbsp** olive oil*
spring onions, chopped
2 fennel bulbs, diced
*20 ml/**4 tsp** tomato purée*
*400 g/**14 oz** canned tomatoes*
*250 ml/**8 fl oz** red wine*
*250 ml/**8 fl oz**/1 cup stock*
*250 ml/**8 fl oz**/1 cup crème fraîche*
*50 g/**2 oz** Wensleydale cheese, crumbled*
*10 ml/**2 tsp** cornflour*
*15 ml/**1 tbsp** cold water*
*30 ml/**2 tbsp** chopped fresh chives*

1 Season the lamb with salt and pepper. Rub in the garlic and herbs.
2 Heat the oil in a pan on a conventional cooker and lightly fry the meat. Add the vegetables, purée and tomatoes. Cover with the wine and stock. Transfer everything to a heat-resistant dish, cover and cook on medium for 40 minutes.
3 Fold in the crème fraîche, cheese and cornflour mixed with water. Cover and heat on full power for 4 minutes. Sprinkle with chives.

Photograph (top)

Venison Steaks

Serves 4
Preparation time: 50 mins
2340 kcal/9595 kJ

8 small venison steaks
salt and freshly ground black pepper
5 ml/*1 tsp* juniper berries, crushed
10 ml/*2 tsp* marjoram
5 ml/*1 tsp* thyme
30 ml/*2 tbsp* olive oil
250 ml/*8 fl oz*/1 cup red wine
250 ml/*8 fl oz*/1 cup gravy
30 ml/*2 tbsp* redcurrant jelly
1 onion, chopped
200 g/*7 oz* oyster mushrooms, diced
250 ml/*8 fl oz*/1 cup cream
30 ml/*2 tbsp* kirsch
50 g/*2 oz* blue cheese, crumbled
30 ml/*2 tbsp* chopped fresh parsley
15 ml/*1 tbsp* redcurrants

1 Rub steaks with salt, pepper, spices and herbs.
2 Heat the oil in a browning dish full power for 2 minutes. Add the steaks and brown on full power for 3 minutes on each side. Cover with the red wine and gravy. Add the jelly, onion, mushrooms and cream, cover and cook on medium for 25 minutes. Season with salt and pepper. Mix in the kirsch and cheese. Cover and cook on full power for 3 minutes. Garnish with parsley and redcurrants.

Photograph (bottom)

Braised Veal Steaks

Serves 4
Preparation time: 45 mins
1480 kcal/6070 kJ

---

4 veal steaks

salt and freshly ground black pepper

5 ml/1 tsp sage

5 ml/1 tsp basil

30 ml/2 tbsp olive oil

2 garlic cloves, crushed

1 onion, chopped

2 carrots, sliced

1 stick celery, sliced

250 ml/8 fl oz/1 cup white wine

400 g/14 oz canned tomatoes

250 ml/8 fl oz/1 cup gravy

100 g/4 oz canned mushrooms, drained

5 ml/1 tsp grated lemon rind

30 ml/2 tbsp chopped fresh parsley

---

1 Rub meat with salt, pepper, spices and herbs.
2 Heat the oil in a frying pan on a conventional cooker and brown the steaks on both sides. Add the garlic and vegetables and cook slowly until soft.
3 Transfer to a heat-resistant dish. Add the wine, tomatoes and gravy. Mix in the mushrooms and flavour with lemon rind. Cover and cook on medium for 25 to 30 minutes. Season and sprinkle with parsley.

Photograph opposite (top)

Chicken Legs with Vegetables

Serves 4
Preparation time: 40 mins
1720 kcal/7050 kJ

---

4 chicken legs

salt and freshly ground black pepper

100 g/ 4 oz/1 cup plain flour

45 ml/3 tbsp salad oil

30 ml/2 tbsp butter or margarine

1 green chilli pepper, deseeded and chopped

1 onion, chopped

1 red pepper, diced

1 green pepper, diced

1 small courgette, sliced

75 g/3 oz stuffed olives

250 ml/8 fl oz/1 cup gravy

250 ml/8 fl oz/1 cup red vermouth

90 ml/6 tbsp crème fraîche

a pinch of sugar

30 ml/2 tbsp chopped fresh chives

---

1 Season the chicken with salt and pepper and coat with flour. Heat the oil in a frying pan on a conventional cooker, add the chicken and brown all over.
2 Place the butter or margarine in a heat-resistant glass or porcelain dish and melt on full power for 1 minute. Add the chilli pepper, onion, the red and green peppers, courgette and well-drained olives. Arrange the chicken legs on top, pour over the gravy and vermouth, cover and cook on medium for 20 to 25 minutes.
3 Add the crème fraîche, season with salt, pepper and sugar, cover and cook on full power for a further 5 minutes.
4 Arrange the chicken legs on a platter, cover with sauce and serve sprinkled with chives.

Photograph opposite (bottom)

Desserts

You can prepare all kinds of tempting desserts in the microwave to serve to the family every day or to guests on special occasions.

Sweet Noodle Dessert, page 58

Sweet Noodle Dessert

Serves 4
Preparation time: 40 mins
3380 kcal/13860 kJ

---

25 g/1 *oz*/2 tbsp butter

1 apple, sliced

1 pear, sliced

100 g/4 *oz* stoned cherries

200 g/7 *oz* strawberries

50 g/2 *oz*/¹/₂ cup pistachio nuts, chopped

50 g/2 *oz*/¹/₂ cup walnuts, chopped

30 ml/2 *tbsp* maraschino

30 ml/2 *tbsp* caster sugar

400 g/14 *oz* ribbon noodles, freshly cooked

150 ml/¹/₄ *pt*/²/₃ cup single cream

4 eggs, beaten

15 ml/1 *tbsp* caster sugar

10 ml/2 *tsp* grated lemon rind

200 g/7 *oz* Mozzarella cheese

---

1 Heat the butter on full power for 2 minutes. Add the fruit, cover and cook on full power for 3 minutes.
2 Mix in the nuts, and maraschino, sprinkle with sugar, cover and cook on full power for 3 minutes.
3 Mix the noodles, cream, eggs, sugar and lemon rind and pour on to fruit and nut mixture. Cover and cook on full power for 5 minutes. Lay the cheese on top, cover and cook on full power for 4 minutes.

Photograph page 56

58

Rice Pudding and Cinnamon Apples

Serves 4
Preparation time: 40 mins
3240 kcal/13285 kJ

---

50 g/2 *oz*/¹/₄ cup butter or margarine

2 cooking apples, diced

a pinch of ground cloves

10 ml/2 *tsp* cinnamon

15 ml/1 *tbsp* caster sugar

juice of 1 lemon

175 g/6 *oz*/1 cup raisins

125 g/4 *oz*/1 cup flaked almonds

450 ml/³/₄ *pt*/2 cups apple juice

250 ml/8 *fl oz*/1 cup single cream

50 g/2 *oz* pudding rice

20 ml/4 *tsp* powdered gelatine

60 ml/4 *tbsp* water

300 ml/¹/₂ *pt*/1¹/₄ cups whipping cream, whipped

30 ml/2 *tbsp* Calvados

30 ml/2 *tbsp* raspberry syrup

a pinch of cinnamon

---

1 Put the butter or margarine into a heat-resistant glass or porcelain dish and heat on full power for 2 minutes. Add the apples. Flavour with the cloves, cinnamon, sugar and lemon juice. Add the raisins, flaked almonds, apple juice and the cream. Stir in the rice and sugar to taste. Cover and cook on full power for 12 to 15 minutes.
2 Finally stir in gelatine dissolved in the water and cook on full power for a further 2 minutes. Leave to cool, but before it has completely set, fold in most of the whipped cream, the Calvados and raspberry syrup.
3 Transfer to suitable glasses and leave in the refrigerator to chill completely. Garnish with the reserved cream and the cinnamon.

Photograph opposite

Gourmet Tip
Rice and pasta have the same cooking time in a microwave oven as in a conventional cooker. For every 1 cup of rice, allow 2 cups of water.

Cherry Sauce

Serves 4
Preparation time: 15 mins
1220 kcal/5000 kJ

400 g/*14 oz* Morrello cherries
250 ml/*8 fl oz*/1 cup red wine
30 ml/*2 tbsp* caster sugar
10 ml/*2 tsp* cinnamon
10 ml/*2 tsp* cornflour
30 ml/*2 tbsp* rum
300 ml/*¹/₂ pt*/1¹/₄ cups single cream

1 Cook all the ingredients in a heat-resistant dish on full power for 5 minutes.

Photograph (top right)

Chocolate Sauce

Serves 4
Preparation time: 20 mins
2200 kcal/9020 kJ

100 g/*4 oz* olain chocolate, grated
150 ml/*¹/₄ pt*/²/₃ cup whipping cream
30 ml/*2 tbsp* white rum
5 ml/*1 tsp* cinnamon
50 g/*2 oz*/¹/₂ cup chopped pistachio nuts
50 g/*2 oz*/¹/₃ cup raisins

1 Cook all the ingredients in a heat-resistant dish on full power for 5 minutes, stirring frequently. Serve with ice cream.

Photograph (bottom right)

Raspberry Sauce

Serves 4
Preparation time: 20 mins
1960 kcal/8035 kJ

10 ml/*2 tsp* cornflour
150 ml/*1/4 pt*/*2/3 cup* cream
30 ml/*2 tbsp* caster sugar
250 ml/*8 fl oz*/1 cup orange juice
250 g/*9 oz* raspberries
30 ml/*2 tbsp* raspberry liqueur

1 Blend the cornflour with the cream and cook with the remaining ingredients, on full power for 5 minutes. Decorate.

Photograph (right)

Orange Sauce

Serves 4
Preparation time: 30 mins
1720 kcal/7050 kJ

4 oranges
30 ml/*2 tbsp* caster sugar
250 ml/*8 fl oz*/1 cup orange juice
juice of 1 lemon
250 ml/*8 fl oz* white wine
50 g/*2 oz*/1 1/2 cup chopped pistachio nuts
30 ml/*2 tbsp* orange liqueur
6 mint leaves, chopped

1 Peel 1 orange thinly then cut the peel into narrow strips. Segment* the oranges.
2 Cook all the ingredients on full power for 5 minutes.

Photograph (bottom left)

61

Pancakes with Nut Filling

Serves 4
Preparation time: 35 mins
3140 kcal/12875 kJ

For the batter:
100 g/4 oz/1 cup flour
2 eggs
250 ml/8 fl oz/1 cup single cream
30 ml/2 tbsp butter or margarine, melted
a pinch of salt
10 ml/2 tsp caster sugar
butter or margarine for greasing .

For the filling:
150 g/5 oz chocolate hazelnut spread
15 ml/1 tbsp orange liqueur
50 g/2 oz/¹/₂ cup walnuts, chopped
50 g/2 oz/¹/₂ cup ground almonds
50 g/2 oz/¹/₂ cup hazelnuts, chopped
50 g/2 oz/¹/₂ cup pistachio nuts, chopped
30 ml/2 tbsp crème fraîche

1 Sift flour into a bowl. Gradually beat in the eggs, cream and melted butter or margarine. Beat steadily until smooth, then stir in the salt and sugar. Grease 4 dessert plates and spread 3 to 4 dessert spoons of batter evenly over each. Cover and cook individually on full power for 3 minutes. Keep the finished crêpes warm.

2 To make the filling, beat the chocolate spread with the orange liqueur until smooth. Fold in the nuts and crème fraîche.
3 Spread the nut filling on to the crêpes and roll each up. Cook each one on full power for a further 2 minutes and serve immediately.

Photograph opposite (top)

Gourmet Tip
It is easy to make pancakes in a microwave. The filling can be varied to suit your own taste. It can be improved with jam or jelly, with brandy or orange liqueur. Instead of chocolate spread, use jam, jelly, fruit purée, bananas and honey or shop-bought syrups and sauces to taste.

Marzipan Apples

Serves 4
Preparation time: 20 min
2020 kcal/8280 kJ

4 cooking apples
juice of 1 lemon
30 ml/2 tbsp Calvados
375 ml/13 fl oz/2 cups cide
30 ml/2 tbsp honey
100 g/4 oz marzipan
50 g/2 oz/¹/₄ cup icing sugar
50 g/2 oz/¹/₂ cup pistachio nuts, chopped
50 g/2 oz/¹/₂ cup pine kernels, chopped
30 ml/2 tbsp orange liqueu
chocolate cream sauce (see page 62)

1 Halve the apples ar hollow out the centre Sprinkle the insides wi lemon juice and Ca vados. Arrange in a hea resistant dish. Mix t gether the cider ar honey and pour over th apples. Cover and coo on full power for minutes.
2 Work the icing sug into the marzipan wi most of the pistachio nu and pine kernels and t orange liqueur. Pack in the apple cavities, cov and cook on full power f a further 5 minutes. Co with chocolate crea sauce and the reserve pistachio nuts and pi kernels before serving.

Photograph opposite (bottom)

Index of Recipes

foulsham
Yeovil Road, Slough, Berkshire, SL1 4JH

ISBN 0-572-01810-X

This English language edition copyright
© 1993 W. Foulsham & Co. Ltd
Originally published by Falken-Verlag,
GmbH, Niedernhausen TS, Germany
Photographs copyright © Falken Verlag

Printed in Portugal